Decorative & Dress Fashion

A. LAMB
50 Blanchland Avenue
Newton Hall
Durham

by the same author
Modern Dressmaking

by the same author
Modern Dressmaking

Decorative &Dress &Fashion

Gwyneth Watts

Hutchinson

London   Melbourne   Sydney   Auckland   Johannesburg

Hutchinson & Co. (Publishers) Ltd

An imprint of the Hutchinson Publishing Group

17–21 Conway Street, London W1P 6JD

Hutchinson Group (Australia) Pty Ltd
30–32 Cremorne Street, Richmond South, Victoria 3121
PO Box 151, Broadway, New South Wales 2007

Hutchinson Group (NZ) Ltd
32–34 View Road, PO Box 40–086, Glenfield, Auckland 10

Hutchinson Group (SA) (Pty) Ltd
PO Box 337, Bergvlei 2012, South Africa

First published 1984

Set in VIP Optima by D. P. Media Limited, Hitchin, Hertfordshire

Printed and bound in Great Britain by
Anchor Brendon Ltd,
Tiptree, Essex

British Library Cataloguing in Publication Data
Watts, Gwyneth
    Decorative dress and fashion.
    1. Dressmaking – Manuals
    I. Title
    646.4'3204   TT515

ISBN 0 09 154271 5

Photograph acknowledgements

Gina Fratini collection, photographer Roger
Eaton, page 1; Camera Press London, pages
2-7, photographers: Femina (pages 2, 4, 6
bottom right, 7 top right); Charlotte Karch
(page 3); Stig Forsberg (page 5); Ernst Wirz
(page 6 *top left*); John Garrett (page 7
bottom left); Pronuptia, photographer
Lee Higham, (page 8).

CONTENTS

PREFACE

This book has been written as a development of my earlier book *Modern Dressmaking*. Dress decoration is given very little place in most books concerned with dressmaking and I see a need to bring this subject together in book form.

The decorative feature of any garment gives it individuality. In some form or other, decoration is always an integral part of up to date fashion in both day and evening wear. I hope that readers will find inspiration to develop this art, and to incorporate their ideas into individual designs.

The contents of this book give instruction and working drawings for different forms and uses of decoration. Fashion illustrations are included to suggest ideas in the various uses of decorative features on a number of garments.

This book should prove useful to students studying on courses in CGLI Creative Studies Fashion Parts I and II, GCE Advanced level dress, CGLI leisure courses in dressmaking and for all students of dress. It should also be of considerable use to the home dressmaker using commercial patterns and be the means of creating garments to personal tastes by the addition of something decorative to the basic design.

I wish to take this opportunity of thanking my colleagues: Tricia Duffy for reading the text, Janette Thistlethwaite for typing the text, and Doug Fox, Paula Bayne and Anne Howes of Hutchinson for all their help.

Gwyneth Watts

INTRODUCTION

There are two different types of dress decoration: structural and applied.

Structural decoration is worked into the construction of a garment so that as the garment is being made up, the decorative feature becomes evident.

Decorative seams are used for this purpose, such as a piped seam used to emphasize a yoke line, or a slot seam given a different coloured or textured backing in order to emphasize a style line.

Pockets, too, fall into this category if they are set into a garment. The making of pockets is not included in this book as the various working methods are covered adequately in *Modern Dressmaking*. A number of decorative features can

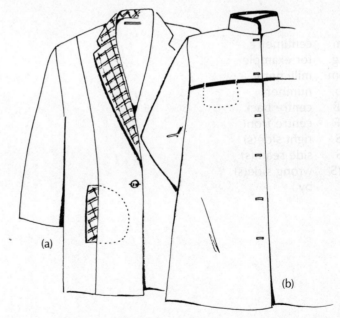

Figure 1   (a) *Welt pocket set into panel seam using checked and plain fabric*
          (b) *Pocket set into piped yoke line using a contrasting or toning coloured piping*

be used in the form of a pocket by the various uses of colour and texture contrast (see Figure 1).

Applied decoration is worked on to a garment to give a variety of attractive finishes. The following chapters present different forms of decoration and give the basic techniques necessary for the working of the decoration.

The fashion illustrations in this book suggest ways in which the decoration can be incorporated into a garment design. These illustrations can be the means of developing further ideas and to extend them into the art of decorative detail.

ABBREVIATIONS

cm	centimetre
e.g.	for example
mm	millimetre
no.	number
CB	centre back
CF	centre front
RS	right side(s)
SS	side seam(s)
WS	wrong side(s)
×	by

Chapter 1

IDEAS, BALANCE, PROPORTION, PREPARATION

Ideas suitable for decorative features are to be found almost anywhere. Natural objects, flower and plant life, fruits and vegetables, rock strata, buildings and landscapes are just some of the sources of inspiration used to bring colour, shape and texture to a design.

Once the decorative feature has been formed it must then be considered in relation to proportion and balance with the part of the garment it is to decorate. Its relation to the whole garment must also be considered, looking at the garment in 'the round', taking back and side views into consideration as well as the front view.

Too heavy or too garish a decoration in size, colour or texture will overpower a garment giving it a cluttered look, and detract from its elegance, as Figure 2 shows.

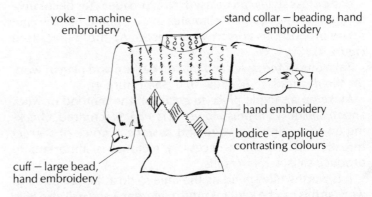

Figure 2 *Blouse in polyester crêpe with decorative features giving a cluttered look*

Any decorative detail must be looked at in its 'total', whether it is incorporated into a part of a garment such as a yoke, collar or cuffs, or whether it runs throughout the length of the garment from the neck to the hem line. It should be

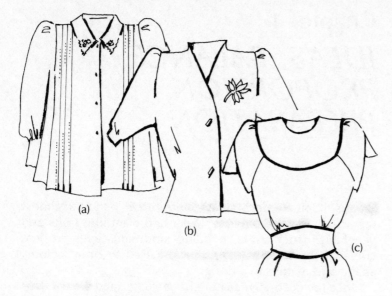

Figure 3   (a) *Pin-tucking bodice decoration*
             (b) *Appliqué in texture contrast*
             (c) *Piped seams on yoke line and belt*

placed so that it draws attention to the wearer's good features. It is a good idea to experiment with design and decorative techniques before attempting to work on a garment.

Basic dress styles can be used to record ideas for decorative features. Using fashion templates as an outline helps to get figure proportions correct when recording these ideas (see Figure 3).

Take one of the styles and make a pattern and plan of work for the decoration in actual size (see Figure 4).

Make up a sample piece to establish the method of work and to decide if the finished result is what is required, checking on size, colour, texture and balance. Choice of correct threads and any other necessary material is important to produce satisfactory results.

It is worthwhile spending the time to do a sample piece of work as this can be kept for future reference and will also give confidence to go ahead and work the decoration on the garment.

There are various ways of transferring the decorative detail to the fabric and these are referred to in the following chapters.

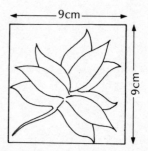

Figure 4   *Appliqué decoration*

Chapter 2
DECORATIVE SEAMS

slot seam

piped seam

top stitching

Figure 5

Seams are used to join one piece of a garment to another in order to assemble the complete garment and to produce particular style lines. In this way seams are functional, but at the same time they can be decorative, emphasizing line, colour and texture contrast (see Figure 5).

Top stitched seam

An open seam, top stitched, gives a smart classic decorative trim emphasizing a style line. The seam allowances can be pressed to one side then top stitched on the right side 0.5 cm from the seam line (see Figure 6). The seam can be pressed open then double top stitched on the RS (see Figure 7).

The machine stitching lines must be accurate. Space the row of stitching 0.5 cm each side of the seam line. The top stitching can be varied to give different effects to the finish:

1 *Straight stitching* Using a stitch length 8–10 stitches to 2.5 cm. For a bold finish, use a buttonhole twist. Alternatively, thread the top of the machine using two spools of thread passing the double thread through the eye of the needle (see Figures 6 and 7).
2 *Twin needle* Using this special needle gives two rows of stitching (see Figure 8(a)).
3 *Embroidery stitches* Patterned stitches forming a straight row of decorative stitching (see Figure 8(b)).

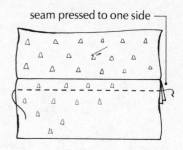

Figure 6

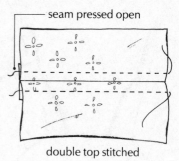

Figure 7

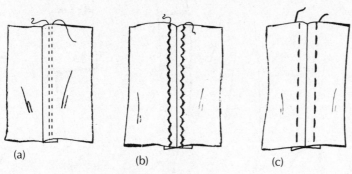

(a)   (b)   (c)

Figure 8   (a) *Twin needle top stitching*
           (b) *Machine embroidery*
           (c) *Saddle stitching*

4 *Saddle stitching* Hand finish. Work with buttonhole thread, form the stitches 0.3–0.5 cm long and evenly spaced (see Figure 8(c)).

These stitches are all illustrated in Figure 9.

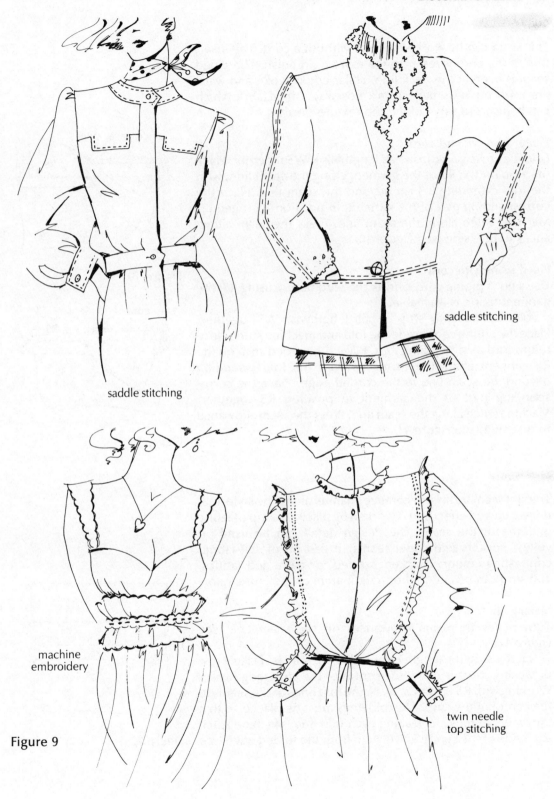

saddle stitching

saddle stitching

machine
embroidery

twin needle
top stitching

Figure 9

Piped seam

This seam can be worked with or without a cord. The insertion of the cord gives a seam a more rigid finish. The piped seam is used at the neck line, collar edges, yoke and waist lines. The piping is made from a crossway strip of fabric which can be used to vary colour and texture finishes.

Piped seam without cord

Fold the crossway strip in half lengthwise, WS together. Place the strip on the RS of the garment along the seam line, with the fold extending 0.3 cm beyond the seam line. Place the corresponding part of the garment in position RS together. Machine stitch along the seam line. Press the seam allowances to one side (see Figure 10).

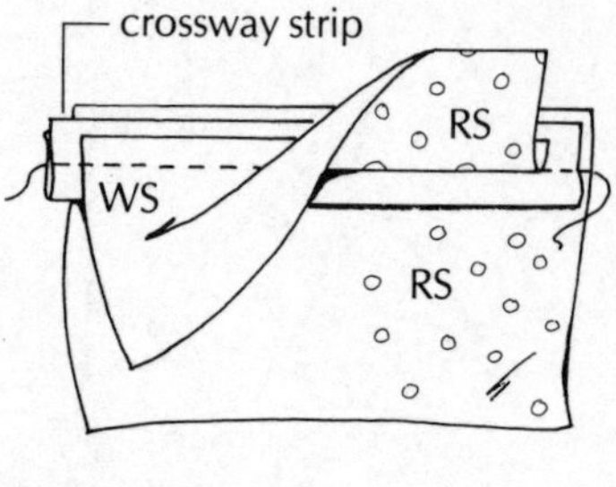

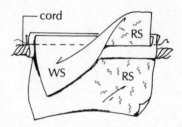

Figure 10

Piped seam with cord

Use a no. 1 piping cord. Shrink the cord before using it if the garment fabric is washable.

Fold the crossway strip in half lengthwise WS together. Place the piping cord inside the fold and machine stitch close to the cord using a piping foot. Place the corded strip on the RS garment along the seam line with the fold extending beyond the seam line to the corded edge. Place the corresponding part of the garment in position RS together. Machine stitch along the seam line. Press the seam allowance to one side (see Figure 11).

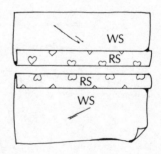

Figure 11

Slot seam

The slot seam forms a decorative channel along the style line. It has a tucked effect and is worked by placing a strip of fabric underneath the seam. The design detail can be used on yokes, pockets and panel seams; it can be of self-fabric, contrasting colour, checked, striped, or patterned fabrics. The strip can be cut on the straight grain or the crossgrain.

Making up

Turn under the seam allowances on the seam line (see Figure 12).

Cut the strip the length required × 4 cm wide. Place a row of tacking stitches down the centre of the strip lengthwise. Working with RS upwards, place the fold lines of the seams to the centre of the strip. The fold lines must be placed so that they meet exactly. Tack along each fold line. Machine stitch each side of the centre line 0.5 cm from the folded edge (see

Figure 12

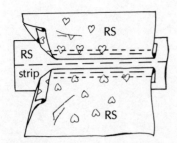

Figure 13

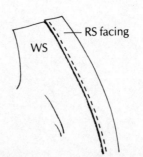

Figure 14

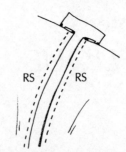

Figure 15

Figure 13). Remove tacking stitches and press.

A slot seam worked on a curved seam must be faced back and the strip must be cut on the same grain as the garment pieces (see Figures 14 and 15).

Chapter 3
APPLIQUÉ

Appliqué is a method of decorating a garment to bring a vivid, subtle, toning or contrasting colour design or texture combinations to give exciting effects. This form of decoration is widely used on a number of garments ranging from children's wear, leisure wear and day wear to evening wear. Delicate work of this type gives lingerie an enchanting individual finish. Appliqué is formed by applying one material to another and there are two ways of using this decoration – *onlaid* or *inlaid* – depending upon the fabric being worked and also the effect required.

The success and beauty of appliqué lies in well-planned design. However simple, the design must be correct in size, balance, proportion, surface detail and colour. Bold shapes with simple outlines lend themselves to this form of decoration. Experiment and practice are necessary before attempting a complicated piece of work.

The decorative stitching which attaches the applied fabric to the ground fabric can be worked by machine or by hand.

Onlaid work

Machine appliqué method
Plan the full design on a sheet of plain paper. Outline each shape in a different coloured pencil (see Figure 16).

Trace off each individual shape and cut out. The shapes are used as patterns for cutting out the fabric pieces (see Figure 17).

Figure 16

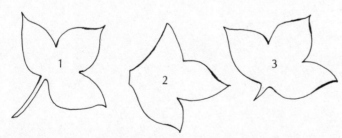

Figure 17

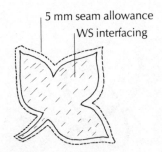

5 mm seam allowance
WS interfacing

Figure 18

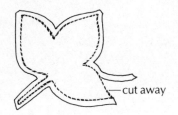

cut away

Figure 19

Figure 20

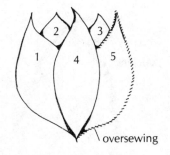

oversewing

Figure 21

Place the pattern pieces on to the fabrics used to build up the appliqué. Cut out, allowing 5 mm beyond the outline. Using a fabric marker, draw in the outline of each pattern shape. This will show clearly the stitching line to follow as each piece is applied.

Cut out each piece in transparent iron-on interfacing without the 5 mm allowance. Press the interfacing to the WS of each piece (see Figure 18). The fabric pieces are now ready to build up the decoration on the ground fabric.

Arrange each piece in its correct position on the ground fabric and tack in place as the design is being built up. Set the sewing machine to straight stitch, setting the length to 12 stitches per 2.5 cm. Using matching thread, stitch carefully on the outline of each piece to secure the appliqué to the ground fabric. Cut away the 5 mm allowance as close to the stitching line as possible (see Figure 19).

Set the sewing machine to zig-zag stitch, setting the width to 1.5–2 and the length to 0.5–1, depending upon the weight of the fabric being worked. Test the stitching for a close satin stitch, varying the length and width of the stitch until the density and size of the stitch is suitable for the fabric being used. Work carefully round the design keeping the lines smooth and even (see Figure 20).

The width of the decorative stitching can be varied to fit in with a design, for example for a flower design, a narrow width for small petals and a wide width for large petals.

A second row of satin stitch directly on top of the first one gives a bold outline to the design. Make this stitch slightly wider than the first row of stitching.

Handwork appliqué
Prepare the design pieces as for machine appliqué, but cut each piece without the 5 mm allowance. Back each piece on the WS with transparent iron-on interfacing. Arrange each piece in its correct position on to the ground fabric and tack in place. Oversew all the cut edges with matching thread using neat, firm stitches (see Figure 21).

The decorative stitches are now worked, covering the outline of the design. A variety of stitches may be used, but to be successful the work must be firm and the stitches close to give a strong outline.

Examples of suitable stitches are as follows:

Satin stitch
Bring the thread out at the left-hand side of the outline, take the stitch over to the right side and bring out again at the

left-hand side close to the stitch previously formed. The stitch width can be varied according to the design being worked (see Figure 22).

Chain stitch

Work with the edge of the outline towards you. Bring the needle up through the work on the outline and insert it again at the same spot. Bring the needle up through the fabric a little further along the outline, keeping the thread under the needle as it is being pulled through. Repeat this process along the outline, keeping the stitches an even length. Do not pull the stitches tightly but allow them to lie flat along the outline (see Figure 23).

Figure 22   *Satin stitch*

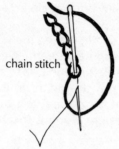
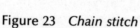

Figure 23   *Chain stitch*   Figure 24   *Herringbone stitch*

Herringbone stitch

Work at two levels taking a stitch at one side of outline and then at the lower side of outline. The needle always comes out in line with the beginning of the previous stitch, and by repeating this process, criss-cross stitches are formed (see Figure 24).

Loop stitch

Work with the edge of the outline towards you. Put the needle into the applied piece a little way from the outline edge and point it towards you. Loop the thread under the needle and pull the needle through to form a loop. The loop sits exactly on the outline edge to give a firm finish. Work the stitches fairly close together (see Figure 25).

Couching

Embroidery threads are laid along the outline of the appliqué and fastened down with small stitches using an independent thread. A single thread, or a number of threads, can be used, depending upon the finish required. Couching can be used

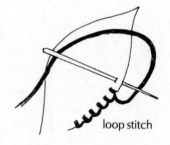

Figure 25   *Loop stitch*

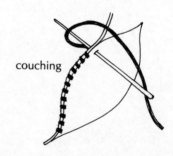

Figure 26   *Couching*

to cover an outline of an applied motif on very fine fabrics, for example lingerie, as the threads lie on the surface of the fabric and therefore will not damage the fine yarns of the fabric. The threads can be matching, or contrasting to give a varied finish. A fine matching thread used to fasten down the laid threads will give an almost invisible finish.

Bring the laid threads through the fabric from the underside to the topside exactly on the outline. Tie them down with a single independent thread.

Follow the outline with the ground threads, guiding them along the line with the left hand. Place the tying-down stitches at regular intervals (3–5 mm apart) and pull fairly tight. The distance between the stitches depends upon the appliqué design. Bring the tying-down stitches closer together at acute corners or narrow curves (see Figure 26).

It is essential to practise embroidery stitches to create a pleasing finish and to give individuality to any decorative work.

Inlaid work

This form of decoration gives a totally different effect in that the contrasting fabric shows through from the underside to the top side of the fabric.

A very fine delicate decoration to lingerie can be worked by machine or hand stitching using contrasting fabrics, lace, or embroidered motifs.

Figure 27   Figure 28

Method
Prepare the design in the usual way. Cut out the separate pieces adding a 5 mm allowance all round each shape. *Do not interface*.

Tack the RS of the pieces to the WS of the fabric and machine or hand stitch round the outline of the shape (see Figure 19). Trim away the 5 mm allowance (see Figure 19). Cut away the fabric on the topside of the motif as close to the outline as possible (see Figure 27).

Working on the RS, machine satin stitch or hand embroider round the edges of the motif (see Figure 28).

Note: Any surface decoration to the applied pieces, for example leaf veins, must be done before the motif is applied to the ground fabric. Figure 29 shows examples of surface decorations.

Figure 29

Chapter 4
PATCHWORK

Figure 30 *Silk taffeta evening coat*

Small geometric shapes of fabric can be stitched together either by hand or by machine to create attractive decorative detail in different ways and on many types of garment and accessories (see Figures 30 and 31).

Materials

Fabrics used to make up a patchwork decorative detail must balance with the rest of the garment. If the weights of the fabrics vary too much the garment could easily be pulled out of shape. Attention must be paid to colour so that the patches are designed and placed to give a pleasing effect. Place the patches in such a way that the lighter or deeper shades harmonize when placed in a certain order. Introduce strong colours to give a dramatic effect.

Method

The patchwork design is built up by using templates made to different geometric shapes (see Figure 32). Templates are available from needlecraft shops. They are made of metal and come in various shapes and sizes. Alternatively, cardboard templates can easily be made by drawing the shapes accurately to the size required and then cutting them out in a firm cardboard. Trace off the templates on to thick paper and cut out a number of shapes to build up the design.

Figure 31 *Patchwork belt*

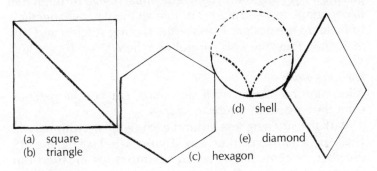

(a) square
(b) triangle
(c) hexagon
(d) shell
(e) diamond

Figure 32

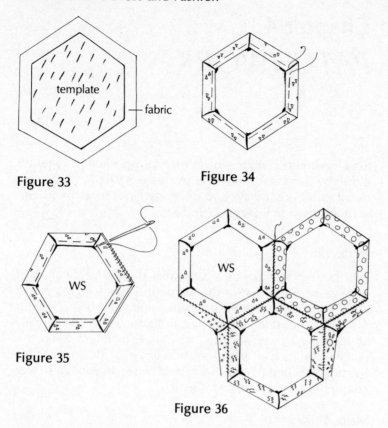

Figure 33

Figure 34

Figure 35

Figure 36

Handwork

Use the paper patches to cut out the fabric adding a 0.5 cm seam allowance (see Figure 33).

Turn the fabric seam allowance over the edges of the template and tack down. Prepare all the patches in this way (see Figure 34).

Using a matching colour thread, join the patches together, placing the RS together. The needle must not go through the paper template (see Figure 35). Join all the patches together to build up the design. Remove the tacking stitches and the templates. Press the work carefully on the WS (see Figure 36).

Machine work

Allowing for a 0.5 cm seam allowance, cut out the patches from the cardboard template shapes.

Mark the stitching line around each template with tailor's chalk or a fabric marker (see Figure 37). Placing the RS together, machine stitch the patches into strips and then join the strips together to build up the design (see Figure 38).

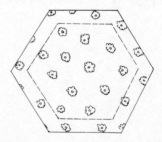

Figure 37

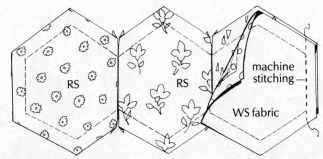

Figure 38

The completed patchwork details can either be stitched into a section of the garment or stitched on to the garment itself (see Figure 39).

Figure 39   (a) *Wool crêpe, satin patchwork at waist and hem line*
(b) *Cotton satin contrasting shades, patchwork yoke and sleeve insertion*

Complete garments can be made from fabric built up into a patchwork design, giving a personal fashion feature (see

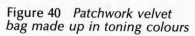

Figure 40   *Patchwork velvet bag made up in toning colours*

Figure 41   *Cotton print patchwork bolero*

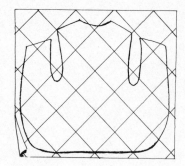

Figures 40 and 41). Build up the patchwork using the same working methods as outlined in Figure 38, making the piece or pieces large enough to fit the pattern (see Figure 42).

Cut out the top pieces and the lining fabric. Make up the garment in the usual way.

Figure 42

Suede patchwork

A variety of suede shapes can be joined together to form exciting colourful designs. However, the skins must be selected carefully so that they are of the same thickness.

Method

Cut out the suede patches placing them together to build up the design (see Figure 43).

Glue the suede pieces carefully on to a calico backing material. Using a zig-zag stitch or an embroidery stitch setting, machine stitch along the edges of the patches (see Figure 44).

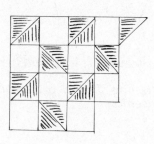

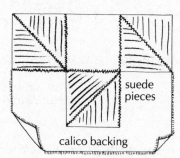

suede pieces

calico backing

Figure 43   **Figure 44**

Figure 45   *Suede sleeveless jacket, patchwork border*

Chapter 5
QUILTING

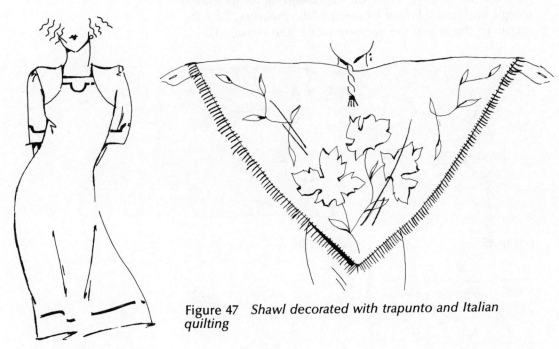

Figure 47 *Shawl decorated with trapunto and Italian quilting*

Figure 46 *Italian quilting at neck line and sleeve edges*

Figure 48 *Machine quilted bolero and skirt*

Quilting is used to give a decorative effect in the form of a raised pattern. Different methods of quilting are used to give different effects (see Figures 46, 47 and 48).

The fabric being worked, the style of the garment, and the area of quilting have to be considered. The raised pattern must have balance and proportion in relation to the position it is being worked on the garment. This must be worked out carefully at the design stage.

Italian quilting

The design motif must be a linear type and must not involve acute angles at any directional turning point.

Material
Top fabric
Matching sewing thread
Muslin (backing material)
Quilting wool (bought in hanks)

Method

Trace off the design on to tracing paper (see Figure 49).

Cut a piece of fine muslin large enough to contain the design (see Figure 50). The muslin is used as a backing material for the quilting. Trace off the design on to the muslin using a fine pencil line or by using a fabric marker. Tack the muslin to the WS of the garment piece (see Figure 51).

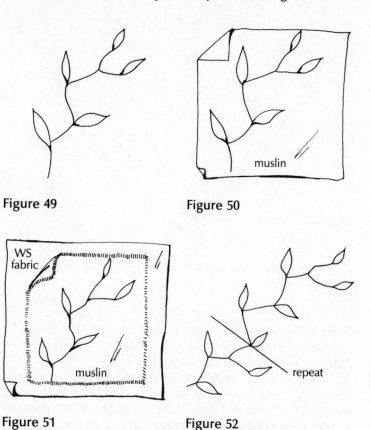

Figure 49   Figure 50

Figure 51   Figure 52

If the design is repeated, trace off the complete design before commencing work (see Figure 52).

Working on the WS, hand stitch, using small running stitches, or machine stitch, each side of the design lines leaving a space of 3 mm between the stitching lines (see Figure 53).

Using quilting wool and a tapestry needle (size 20), thread the wool through the backing material along the channel lines forming the design. Leave a small loop in the wool at regular intervals along the design so that the wool is not

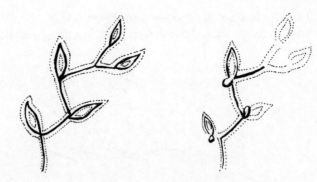

Figure 53   Figure 54

pulled too tightly. The loops formed will also allow for shrinkage of the wool if the garment is to be laundered (see Figure 54).

The threading of the wool through the channels gives a pattern in relief on the RS of the garment (see Figure 46).

Trapunto

The design requires bold shapes and is unsuccessful if attempted on linear work.

Materials
Top fabric
Matching sewing thread
Muslin (backing material)
Quilting wadding (bought in bags by weight)

Method
Trace off the design on to tracing paper (see Figure 55).

Cut a piece of muslin large enough to contain the design (see Figure 56). Trace the design on to the muslin using a fine pencil line, or by using a fabric marker. Tack the muslin to the WS of the garment piece (see Figure 57).

Trace off any repeat design before working (see Figure 58).

Working on the WS of the garment, using small running stitches, or machine stitching, follow the lines of the design.

When the design has been completely outlined fill out the focal points of the pattern with the wadding.

Snip into the centre of the muslin backing. Tease the wadding into the small opening using a little wadding at a time. When sufficient wadding has been inserted to give the raised effect on the RS, draw the snip in the muslin together and

Figure 55

Figure 56

secure it with a few small stitches (see Figure 59).

The padding gives a raised pattern on the RS of the garment (see Figure 47).

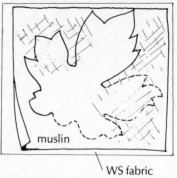

Figure 58

Figure 57

Note: Italian quilting and trapunto can be used together to form interesting designs. Care in creating a design shape is very necessary. Avoid too many small curves in an Italian quilting design as curves make it difficult to thread the wool through evenly. Avoid too large an area in a trapunto design as this makes it difficult to arrive at an evenly filled pattern.

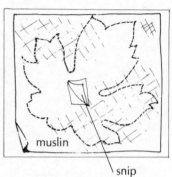

Figure 59

Machine quilting

This form of decoration can be worked in straight lines or random wavy lines, or as in contour quilting, following the outline of a pattern on the fabric surface.

Materials
Top fabric
Matching sewing thread
Lining fabric
Sheet wadding (this type of wadding can be separated to give the required thickness)

Method
Trace off the design on to tracing paper. Transfer the design lines on to the lining fabric. Place the three layers of material together. Tack through all three layers to hold them in place (see Figure 60).

Before commencing to machine stitch the design through all three layers, check the needle size and stitch length required according to the materials being worked. A longer

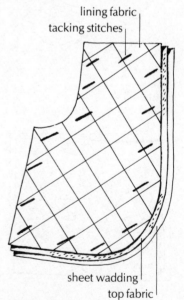

Figure 60

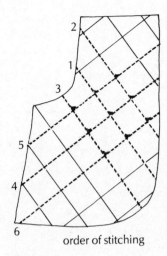

2
1
3
5
4
6
order of stitching

Figure 61

stitch gives a better result than a short stitch length (usual setting is 8–10 stitches to 2.5 cm).

Using a matching or a contrasting coloured thread, stitch along the design lines easing the work to give an even distribution of the wadding. For an all-over quilted section, work from the centre and sides of the material to keep the distribution of the wadding constant (see Figure 61).

When quilting a complete section of a garment such as a yoke, pockets, or cuffs, quilt a piece of material before cutting out the pattern piece. This will help to centralize the design (see Figure 62).

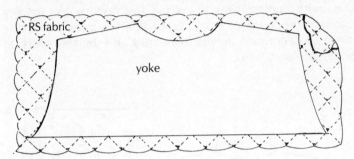

RS fabric

yoke

Figure 62

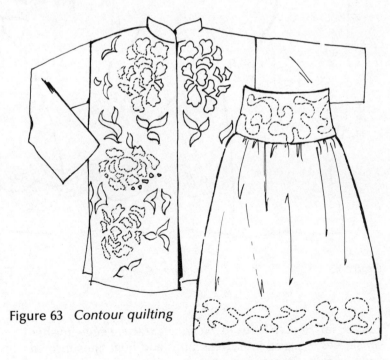

Figure 63 *Contour quilting*

Figure 64 *Random quilting*

Chapter 6
EMBROIDERY

Embroidery is a form of decoration which has a very simple beginning but one which can develop into a form of decoration with endless uses in colour and texture and in very different mediums of work. Embroidery is used in a wide range of decorative details from very fine delicate work to bold encrusted work.

Figure 65   Figure 66   Figure 67

Basic stitches can be used to create attractive edge finishes on sleeves, collars, cuffs, neck lines and hem lines formed from a single row or built up to form a deep border finish (see Figures 65, 66 and 67).

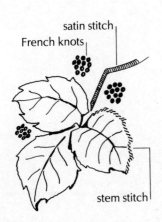

Figure 68

The following points must be considered when choosing embroidery as a garment decoration.

1 The fabric being worked; whether it is washable, hard-wearing, or a delicate lingerie fabric.
2 The part of the garment to be decorated.
3 The stitches and type of embroidery to be worked.
4 The choice of threads.

Experiments with fabrics, stitches and threads must be worked out before working on the actual garment.

Decide upon the purpose of the embroidery. Work out the design to the full size scale so that balance and proportion are maintained. Build up a border pattern or a motif design choosing two or three basic stitches and a good colour combination (see Figure 68).

Design equipment

Cartridge paper – for working out the design detail
Tracing paper – for tracing off the design
2B pencil

Marking equipment

Tracing wheel
Dressmaker's carbon paper
Tailor's chalk
Fabric marker
Pounce powder

There are various ways of transferring the embroidery design to the fabric.

1 Follow the design lines, making a fine outline in small dots with a tracing wheel over the carbon paper (see Figure 69).

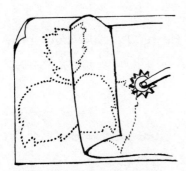

Figure 69

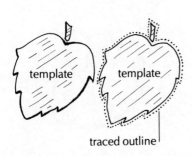

Figure 70

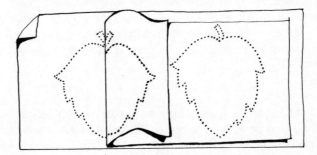

Figure 71

2   Tailor's chalk can be used to trace round cardboard shapes (see Figure 70).
3   Pounce powder is contained in a small coarsely woven bag which is rubbed over a series of perforations along the outline of the design. The perforations can be made by using a tracing wheel along the design lines (see Figure 71).

Hand embroidery

Equipment

Needles
The selection of which needle to use must be made in relation to the fabric being worked and the type of embroidery. The Crewel needle has a long eye which is shaped to allow soft threads to move freely through it. It will also accommodate various thicknesses of threads. The Crewel needle is available in a range of sizes from a coarse needle to a very fine needle.

Threads
A variety of threads and wools are used for fashion embroidery depending upon the type of decoration, the fabric being worked and the type of garment. See Table 1 for a general selection guide.

Working basic stitches

Running stitch
Worked from right to left, this is the simplest stitch. The stitches on the topside of the work must all be the same length. Variations of this stitch can give added interest (see Figure 72).

Stem stitch
This stitch is used as an outline stitch. The stitches are worked from left to right. The needle is brought out close to the last stitch, and the thread must be placed above the needle (see Figure 73).

Chain stitch
This stitch can be used singly as a 'daisy stitch', used as an outline to a design, or used to 'fill' in a design. The stitch is formed by holding the thread on the fabric surface while taking a stitch so that the needle passes *over* the thread to make a loop (see Figure 74).

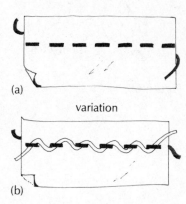

(a)

variation

(b)

Figure 72   (a) *Running stitch*
(b) *Whipped running stitch*

Figure 73   *Stem stitch*

Figure 74   *Chain stitch (daisy)*

Silk taffeta short ballgown with contrast bow-tied sash.

Cross-over dress, showing machine appliqué and hand embroidery of Oriental design.

Table 1 *Thread and wool selection guide*

THREADS	DESCRIPTION	USES
Stranded cotton	Shiny appearance, made up into six fine strands. Can be divided to use as separate strands.	Use two or three strands for fine embroidery on light-weight fabrics. Use six strands for a bold finish.
Soft embroidery	A thick cotton thread with a matt surface	Used for hand embroidery on medium-weight loosely woven fabrics.
Cotton Perlé	Shiny appearance, the yarn has a twist. Sold in spools in two thicknesses: no. 5 and no. 8	Used for hand and machine embroidery on medium and light-weight fabrics according to type of finish required.
Cotton à broder	A medium weight yarn with a matt surface.	Hand embroidery, a firm thread to give a good edge decoration on medium fabrics.
Tapestry wool	A thick wool, sold in small hanks.	Bold embroidery on plain woven fabrics. Canvas work.
Machine embroidery thread	Available in plain and variegated shades. Two thicknesses no. 30 and no. 50.	All types of machine embroidery on light-weight and medium-weight fabrics.
Lurex thread	Available in silver or gold.	Used on the bobbin, with machine embroidery thread in the top threading.

Satin stitch

The stitches are worked close together and run parallel to each other. The stitches can vary in length according to the shape of the design (see Figure 75).

Feather stitch

This is a delicate stitch giving a soft feathery line. The stitch is formed by making loop stitches, alternating the direction to give variety. Stitches can be worked in a single row, or arranged in groups (see Figure 76(a) and (b)).

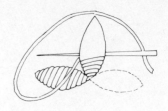

Figure 75   *Satin stitch*

French knots

These stitches are more effective when grouped together. The knot must be firmly secured to give the best effect. Bring the needle through to the topside of the fabric. Hold the thread down with the thumb and twist the thread three times around the needle. Hold the knot firmly, insert the needle through to the underside of the fabric, as near as possible to the starting point. Secure firmly (see Figure 77).

These are just some of the basic stitches that are used to form edge finishes at neck lines, sleeves, belts and hem lines (see Figure 78). They can also be built up to form interesting, exciting decorative detail (see Figure 79).

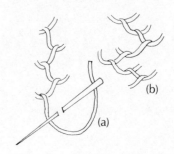

Figure 76   *Feather stitch*

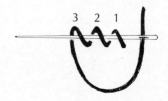

Figure 77   *French knot*

Figure 78   *Feather stitch and French knots on cuff*

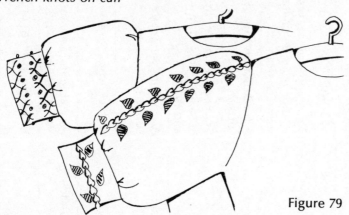

Figure 79

Shadow work

This type of embroidery is used on lingerie and blouses. It gives a very distinctive appearance to a garment. A combination of some basic embroidery stitches is used to work this decoration (see Figure 80). Other embroidery detail forming the design can be worked in stem stitch (see Figure 73).

Shadow work is only suitable to use on transparent or translucent fabrics as the beauty of the embroidery design shows through to the RS from the underside of the fabric. The outline of the design must be simple and must not be too large because of stitch slippage and distortion.

Working method
Plan the design detail, trace on to tracing paper and transfer to the fabric (see Figure 81).

The embroidery is formed by working herringbone stitch from the underside of the fabric. The stitches must be placed very close together and should touch each other. Follow the outline of the given shape exactly, working closely into any pointed area of the design. Back stitches form the outline of the shape on the RS (see Figure 82).

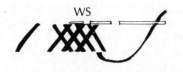

Figure 80 *Close herringbone stitch*

Figure 81 *Design outline*

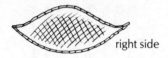

Figure 82 *Back stitch forming the outline of the design*

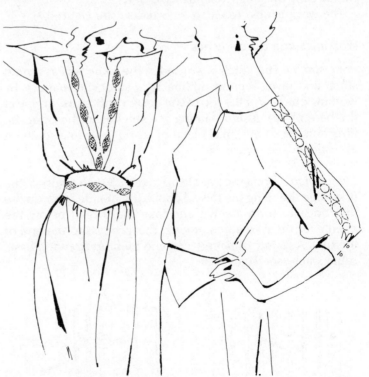

Figure 83 (left) *Nightdress – cotton voile, satin binding, shadow work at neck line and waist*

Figure 84 (right) *Blouse – white polyester georgette with shadow work decoration on sleeve*

Smocking

Smocking is used to hold fullness in a garment in place in a decorative way. It is used on blouses, dresses, lingerie and on children's wear.

There are many traditional smocking patterns to follow giving deep, complex decorative detail, but smocking can also be used by forming a very attractive decoration from a few basic smocking stitches.

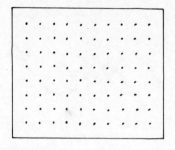

Figure 85

Preparation work

The fabric requirement is three times the finished width of the smocking. Mark the fabric at 0.5 cm intervals by means of a small dot along the width of the fabric and to the required depth of the smocking area (see Figure 85).

Using tacking cotton, work rows of running stitches picking up a small amount of fabric at each dot (see Figure 86). Pull the threads up to form the fabric into small ridges and secure the threads by tying the ends together.

The work is now ready to embroider (see Figure 87).

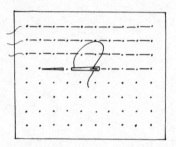

Figure 86

Working some basic stitches

Rope stitch   This stitch is worked in the same way as a stem stitch and gives a good outline to a smocking pattern by working one row at the top of the design and a further row at the base of the design slanting the stitches in the opposite direction. Pick up a small piece of fabric to form a stitch on each ridge (see Figure 88).

Cable stitch   Bring the needle up to the RS of the work at the first ridge. Keeping the thread above the needle, pick up the first ridge to form a stitch and take the thread below the needle for the next stitch. Repeat this process to the end of the row. A variety of patterns can be built up from the basic cable stitch (see Figure 89).

Figure 87

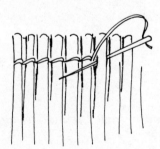

Figure 88   *Rope stitch*

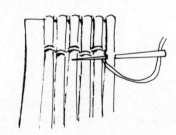

Figure 89   *Cable stitch*

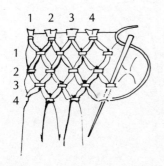

Figure 90 *Honeycomb stitch*

Honeycomb stitch Bring the needle up to the RS of the work at the first ridge. Take a small stitch at the second ridge drawing ridges 1 and 2 together. Bring the needle up at the next row immediately below. Repeat the stitch, bringing ridges 2 and 3 together. Return the needle to the original line through ridge number 3, repeat the stitch bringing ridges 3 and 4 together. Continue to the end of the first two rows then proceed to work on rows 3 and 4 (see Figure 90).

Figure 91 *Smocking*

Figure 92 *Smocking*

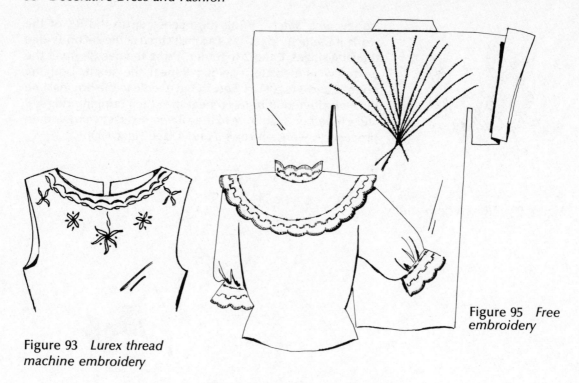

Figure 93   *Lurex thread machine embroidery*

Figure 95   *Free embroidery*

Figure 94   *Machine embroidery*

Machine embroidery

It is necessary to practise various techniques to completely master this skill, but once mastered it offers endless possibilities and a variety of uses. It is a way of adding a decorative detail to a garment giving quick results and a pleasing finish.

Rows of embroidery stitches can form an interesting edge finish (see Figures 93 and 94).

Free embroidery can be used to form floral, geometric and abstract designs, giving an attractive and individual touch as a decorative detail on a garment (see Figure 95).

Automatic machine embroidery

The sewing machine used must be a model able to produce embroidery stitches which are either built into the mechanism, or are produced by the use of 'cams' which are inserted into the machine. The embroidery stitches are formed as the stitching progresses. The given instructions must be followed carefully according to the machine being used.

Many reputable machines are built for this purpose. Any good sewing machine sales outlet will give advice on the machines available.

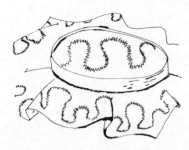

Figure 96   *Embroidery ring*

Free embroidery
It is possible to work this embroidery on any sewing machine.

Experimental work is essential and it is necessary to use an embroidery ring (see Figure 96). Great care must be taken when placing the fabric into the embroidery ring. The fabric must be held taut. If it is slack the machine will miss stitches and the work will become distorted.

Working method
Remove the presser foot from the machine. Thread the machine in the usual way and loosen the top tension slightly. Drop the feed dog; this is done in different ways, depending upon the machine mechanism. The machine manual will give instructions on how it is done. Place the ring underneath the needle position so that the fabric touches the machine bed.

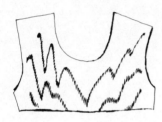

Figure 97   *Free embroidery practice*

Draw the bobbin thread up through the fabric. Hold the upper and lower threads when commencing to work.

Lower the presser foot bar (this is easily forgotten when no presser foot is in position). Always check that the bar is down before commencing to stitch. Run the machine at a medium speed and slowly move the embroidery ring backwards and forwards and from side to side so that the embroidery is built up into a design (see Figure 97).

Practise this exercise, forming lines and shapes at random until complete machine-control is achieved.

Lift the presser foot bar to remove the work.

Chapter 7
SCALLOPS

Figure 98   *Scallops*   Figure 99   *Scallops built in to style line*

Scalloped edges make an attractive finish to a garment giving a soft rounded finish which is flattering to certain garments (see Figure 98).

Cutting

It is essential to have the scallops uniform in size. Measure each scallop accurately. Make a template to use for cutting the edge of the fabric to the shape of the scallops (see Figure 100).

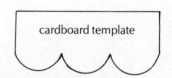

cardboard template

Figure 100   *Cardboard template*

Camisole showing pin tucking and lace insertions. Front fastening with buttons and rouleau ties.

Strapless evening top in sequined fabric. Satin bow-tie with bead and sequin decoration.

Blouse. Scalloped lace edging to lower sleeve edge and front bodice panel.

Long sleeved tunic showing
machine embroidery on front
bodice and at hemline giving
scalloped finish. Belt – woven
contrasting yarns to give diagonal
surface texture. Leather buckle and
trim.

Cotton cambric dress showing
groups of pin tucks from neckline.
Flounce collar with broderie
anglaise edging.

Two wedding dresses in spotted tulle. On the left, asymmetric shoulder line is
accentuated by double frill. Short veil has scalloped edging. On the right, neckline
frill and bouffant sleeves.

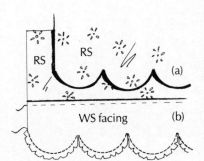

Figure 101

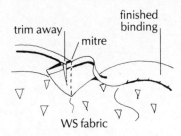

Figure 102

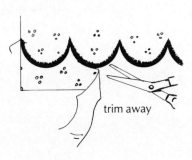

Figure 103

Making up

Neatened with facing

Attach the facing to the garment, placing the RS together, following the lines of the scallops. Pivot the needle at the point of each scallop. Notch at the inner points and at 1.5 cm intervals along the curve of each scallop. Press and turn the facing to the WS. Neaten the outer edge of the facing. Press, taking care to keep the shape of the scallops constant (see Figure 101(a) and (b)).

Neatened with binding

Attach the binding to the RS of the garment, stitching 0.5 cm from the edge, following the line of the scallops. Stretch the binding at the point of each scallop and ease the binding over the curves. Pivot the needle at the point of each scallop. Turn the binding to the WS of the garment and mitre the corner to allow the binding to lie flat. The mitre can be sewn down using small hand-running stitches (see Figure 102).

Machine embroidered edge finish

Choose a curved shaped embroidery stitch. Neaten the scalloped edge with the embroidery. Cut away the excess fabric. Press lightly (see Figure 103).

Scallops loosely attached to a style line

Cut out the fabric and the facing. Make up the scalloped edging as shown in Figure 100.

Turn the work to the RS and press. Tack the work together at the straight edge (see Figure 104).

Attach the scallop decoration to the corresponding garment piece along the fitting line (see Figure 105).

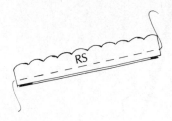

Figure 104

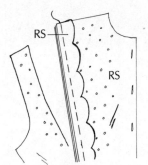

Figure 105

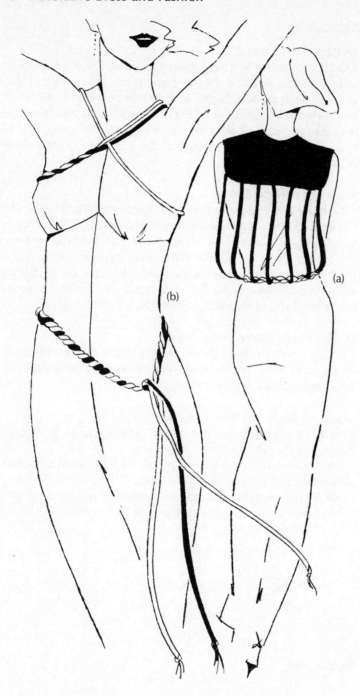

Figure 106   (a) *Rouleau attached to the back yoke and hanging loosely to waist line*
(b) *Rouleau shoe-string straps from bodice style line and a plaited rouleau tie belt*

Chapter 8
ROULEAU

Rouleau means roll. In a dressmaking context it is a tube of fabric made on the true cross to give the tube the maximum amount of stretch so that it may be curved, twisted, plaited or attached over a rounded area in an attractive way (see Figure 106(a) and (b)).

Making rouleau

Cutting
Fold over the fabric at right angles so that the warp threads lie parallel to the weft threads (see Figure 107).

Press a crease into the fabric along the fold line. Using the crease as a guide line, rule off the number of strips required at the width required (see Figure 108). The width will depend upon the type of fabric being used and the form of decoration being worked.

Joining
Trim the strips so that the ends are cut on the straight grain. Place the strips RS together (see Figure 109).

Machine stitch 5 mm from the straight edge and press the seam open. Cut away the protruding triangles. On a long length all the joins must lie in the same direction (see Figure 110).

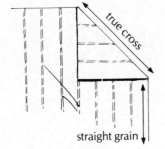

Figure 107

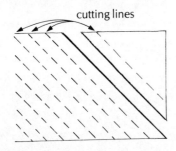

Figure 108

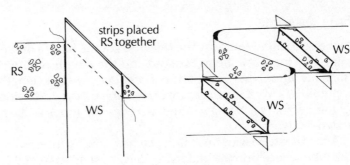

Figure 109
Figure 110

Stitching and pulling through

Fold the strip in half lengthwise with the RS together. Machine stitch 5 mm from the fold line leaving the ends of the strip open. (Take a smaller measurement from the fold to make a narrower tube.) Fasten a thread securely to one end of the tube. Using a bodkin pull through gently to the RS (see Figure 111).

Figure 111

Flat rouleau

To enable the tube to lie flat trim away the seam allowance inside the tube (see Figure 112).

Pull through to the RS. Press the tube, making sure that the seam sits exactly on the edge of the tube.

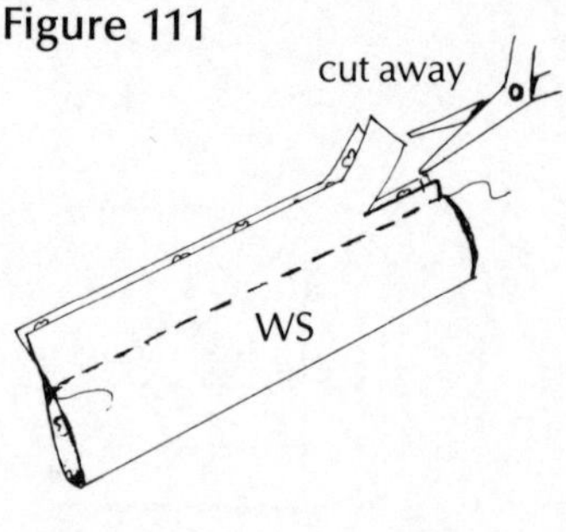

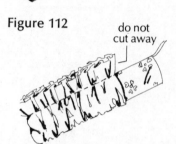

Figure 112

Round rouleau

Pull the tube through to the RS leaving the full seam allowance inside the tube to fill out the centre and so keep it in its rounded shape (see Figure 113).

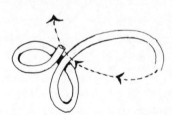

Figure 113

Plaited rouleau

Make up flat rouleau to three times the required length. Three lengths are required to make a 'three plait' (see Figure 160, page 59). Four lengths are required to make a 'four plait' (see Figure 161, page 59).

A variety of different effects can be achieved by use of colour contrast and by using tubes of fabric of different textures, for example satin and crêpe. Make up the plait, and hand sew it to the garment on the underside of the plait.

Rouleau is also used as a decorative fastening on garments and accessories.

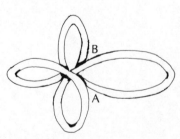

Figure 114

Frog fastening

Make up a round rouleau. The thickness of the tube is determined by the fabric being worked and the length required depends upon the size of the fastening (average length required 30 cm). Keep the seam of the tube on the underside as the fastening is being worked. Arrange the loops as illustrated in Figure 114).

Attach the tube with small firm stitches, sewing the ends of the tube securely on the underside. Secure at points A and B, leaving the main loop free to take up the button (see Figure 115).

Figure 115

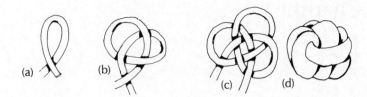

Figure 116

Chinese ball button

Make up a round rouleau. The thickness of the tube controls the size of the button. One button requires a piece of tubing 25 cm long.

Follow diagrams (a) to (d) in Figure 116 which shows how to interlock the loops. Work with the loops open arranging them in the centre of the tube. Keep the ends of the tube together as the button is being shaped. Gently ease the loops in position – do not pull tightly. Fasten the ends securely close to the back of the button. Cut away the excess tubing.

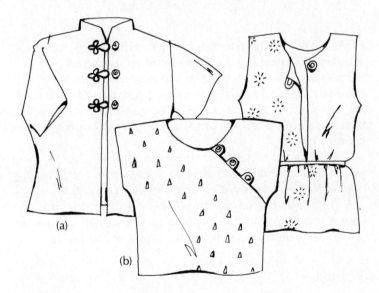

Figure 117   (a) *Frog fastening*
              (b) *Rouleau loops and Chinese ball button*

Chapter 9
TUCKS

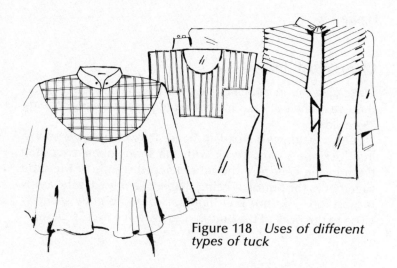

Figure 118 *Uses of different types of tuck*

Tucks are used to hold fullness in place. The type of tuck used will depend upon the amount of control required.

Tucks are always decorative, but how decorative is determined by the fabric and thread being used, whether the tucks are arranged in groups, crossed or scalloped, or whether they are simply used as two or three pin tucks on a blouse front or back.

The placing of tucks is very important. Moving tucks, even by a small amount in one direction or another, can alter the overall line of a decorative detail (see Figure 119).

A firmly woven fabric should be used for tucking and unless a colour contrast is planned the thread used must always be a perfect match to the colour of the fabric.

Method

The extra amount of fabric required to make a tuck is twice the depth of the tuck.

Tucks usually follow the grain of the fabric either vertically or horizontally. Diagonal tucking is best worked on a pattern piece which has been cut on the true cross so that the tucks are stitched on the straight grain.

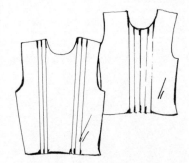

Figure 119 *Different placing of pin tucks to show how the overall effect of the tucking can be altered*

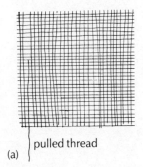

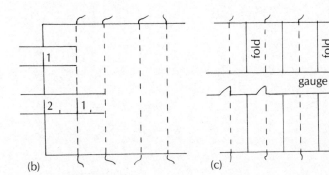

(a) pulled thread

(b)

(c) fold fold gauge

Figure 120

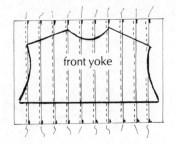

front yoke

Figure 121

Marking

There are various ways of marking tuck positions:

1 Pull one thread from the fabric to mark the folded edge of the tuck (see Figure 120(a)).
2 Measure carefully and trace tack, following the grain line. Mark each tuck accordingly (see Figure 120(b)).
3 Establish the fold line of the first tuck then measure with a cardboard gauge and accurately mark the following tucks by spacing them at uniform distances or in groups (see Figure 120(c)).

It is often practicable to tuck a piece of fabric before cutting out the pattern piece (see Figure 121).

Types of tucks

Tucks can vary in width from 0.2 cm to 5 cm. They are stitched on the RS of the fabric through double fabric and are pressed flat.

A number of variations can be used to give different effects.

Pin tucks

These are very fine tucks approximately 0.2 cm wide. Pin tucks must run in the direction of the grain of the fabric as they will not press correctly if the machine stitching is off grain (see Figure 122).

Crossed tucks

It is better to do this type of tucking before cutting out the pattern piece (as in Figure 121). The tucks must be evenly spaced. Mark and stitch all tucks on the lengthwise grain of

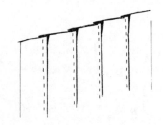

Figure 122 *Pin tucks*

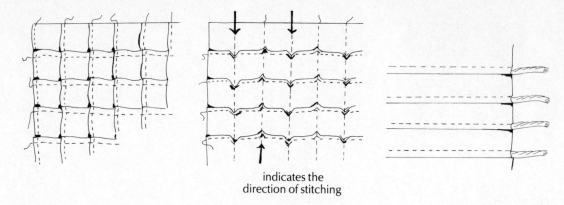

indicates the
direction of stitching

Figure 123   *Crossed tucks*   Figure 124   *Scalloped effect*   Figure 125   *Corded tucks*

the fabric. Press the tucks in one direction. Using the same
spacing, mark and stitch all the tucks on the crosswise grain.
Press the tucks in one direction. The tucked fabric is then
ready for the pattern lay (see Figure 123).

Crossed tucking with a scalloped effect
Work as outlined above for crossed tucks on the lengthwise
grain. When working on the crosswise grain, stitch so that the
pressed tuck is kept flat, then stitch the second row easing
the tuck over to sit in the opposite direction. Continue stitching, alternating the directional stitching of the tucks in each
row (see Figure 124).

Corded tucks
The cord is inserted into the fold of the tuck making it into a
rigid raised line. A coarse crochet cotton is suitable for this
type of tuck.
    Place the cord on the WS of the fabric along the fold line.
Stitch close to the cord using a piping foot (see Figure 125).

Shell tucks
This is a decorative tuck giving a shelled edge effect to the
fold. This type of tuck gives a delicate finish to lingerie (see
Figure 126).
    Mark the stitching line into a series of equally spaced small
dots. The width between the dots gives the size of the shell
formed (the approximate size is 0.5 cm). The tucks are made
with running stitches, using three or four stitches to each
shell. Fold the fabric over to form the tucked edge with the
dots marked 0.3 cm below the fold line.

Figure 126   *Shell tucking on
waist slip*

Victorian nightdresses, tucked bodice gathered into straight neckband. Front decorated with hand embroidery.

Tunic with wide bell sleeves. Lace yoke with shoestring ties at neckline. Tucks on bodice and sleeve edge, lace edging completes the decoration.

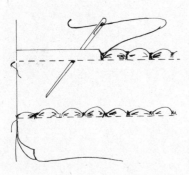

Figure 127 *Shell tucks*

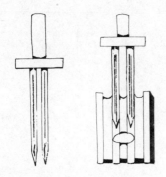

Figure 128 (left) *Twin needle*

Figure 129 (right) *Base of tucking foot*

Figure 132 *Twin needle pin tucking*

Sew the tuck to the first dot. Take the needle over the fold through the stitching line to the back of the tuck. Draw the thread up tightly and work a small back stitch to secure the tuck. Continue the running stitch to the next dot to make the next shell (see Figure 127).

It is also possible to work this form of tucking on certain sewing machines.

Twin needle tucks
These tucks are worked on machines which have a tucking foot attachment. The foot attachment has a number of grooves on its base. A twin needle (two needles mounted to a central bar) should be used (see Figure 128). The needle must be lined up with the grooves on the base of the foot (see Figure 129).

When threading the machine, two spools of thread must be used. Place a thread each side of the tension disc. The machine handbook will give instructions for the correct setting.

The stitch length setting is 12 stitches to 2.5 cm. The width of the machine foot makes a good guide for regular spacing of the tucks. The fabric can be tucked before the pattern piece is cut out.

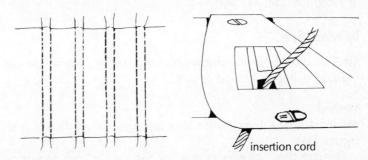

Figure 130   Figure 131

Worked on single fabric, the tucks are formed while being stitched. Machine stitch the first tuck, then space the rows accordingly (see Figure 130). Twin needle tucking forms a ridge similar to the pin tuck and can be used effectively in groups or combined with other types of tuck.

It is possible to 'cord' this type of tuck, by feeding a fine cord up through the foot plate. This gives a firm raised tuck (see Figure 131).

Chapter 10
LACE

Lace has a unique appearance, giving a luxury look to garments. It is different from other fabrics in its construction and
requires different handling skills.

There are many types of lace made up from a variety of
fibres, both natural and synthetic. The thickness of the yarn
used in the construction determines the weight and the uses
of the lace.

1 *Piece lace* Available in different widths and weights,
   used for parts of or complete garments. It is also used for
   applying a single motif decoration.
2 *Lace edgings* Varying from a deep lace of up to 15 cm
   wide to a very narrow 0.5 cm lace edging.
3 *Lace motifs* Made up singly and applied directly on to
   the garment.

See Figures 136, 137 and 138.

Joining lace

The join must be as inconspicuous as possible. The following
method will give a good result.

Method
Mark the fitting lines on the lace using coloured thread (see
Figure 133).

Overlap the lace pieces placing the fitting lines together
(see Figure 134).

Trace along a prominent raised line in the lace pattern
within the overlapped area A (see Figure 134).

Oversew along this line using a matching coloured thread.

Cut away the surplus lace on the topside and on the underside of the join. Press the work lightly on the WS (see Figure
135).

Lace edgings

Turn a very narrow hem to the RS of edge to be trimmed.

Arrange the straight edge of the lace over the hem, placing

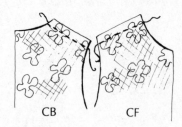

CB   CF

Figure 133

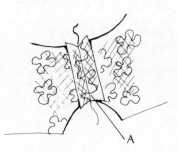

A

Figure 134

Figure 135

Figure 136 *Lace edged negligée découpé at hem line*

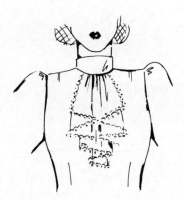

Figure 137 *Lace edged jabot*

Figure 138 *Bridal wear*

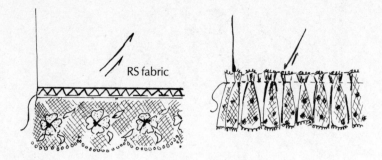

Figure 139   Figure 140

the lace on the RS to cover the raw edge of the fabric. Using a narrow zig-zag machine stitch setting, attach the edging to the garment (see Figure 139).

For a fuller frilled edging the lace can be gathered slightly. Most lace edgings have a thread running through the straight edge which can be pulled easily to gather the lace. Gather the lace gently, adjusting the gathers evenly (see Figure 140).

Apply the lace using a narrow zig-zag machine stitch setting.

Patterned edging

Lay the corded edge of the lace over the edge of the garment allowing sufficient overlap to take the shape of the lace pattern. Tack the lace into position. Using a narrow zig-zag machine stitch setting, attach the lace to the fabric along the corded patterned edge (see Figure 141). Trim away the fabric from the underside.

Working with a double-sided lace edging, this method can be used for lace insertion.

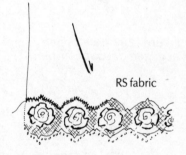

Figure 141

Lace appliqué

The pattern of the lace must be chosen carefully to give a suitable motif for application. Make sure that the motif has a clearly defined raised pattern line.

Method

Cut out the lace centralizing the motif. Place the lace on to the RS of the fabric, RS uppermost. Tack into position (see Figure 142).

Figure 142

Figure 143   Figure 144

Handwork
Proceed to oversew around the raised outline of the motif, placing the stitches so that they touch each other (this is important as the work must be strong enough to withstand washing).

Complete the hand sewing, then cut away the surplus lace around the motif (see Figure 143).

Machine work
Tack the lace into position (see Figure 142). Set the machine to a narrow zig-zag stitch setting (width 1.5; length 1).

Machine stitch around the outline of the motif. Cut away the surplus lace around the motif (see Figure 143).

Lace découpé

Work as for lace appliqué, cutting away the surplus lace on the RS of the work. Working on the underside, cut away the fabric underneath the attached motif so that the openwork design of the motif is seen from both sides of the work (see Figure 144).

Figure 145 *Camisole – lace découpé skirt with lace edged frill*

Chapter 11
BEADING

Beading brings an unexpected look of luxury to a garment. A wide variety of beads of different shapes, sizes, colours and surface textures are available and from which, exciting patterns can be formed to produce an elegant decoration. The beadwork can be built up over padding to give a three-dimensional effect which is particularly attractive on stand collars, belts and evening bags (see Figures 146 and 147).

Figure 146 *Satin beaded evening bag*

Equipment and materials

Needles
Beading needles must be used. They are very fine and flexible made from soft steel, and they are longer than a normal sewing needle.

Thread
Use no. 50 sewing thread, which can be waxed lightly by rubbing with beeswax. This prevents the thread from twisting and breaking.

Backing material
Support the beading by placing a fabric such as organdie or muslin on the underside of the garment piece, to which the beads are to be applied.

Figure 147 *Beaded collars*

Beads
Seed	These are very small and round.
Bugle	These are long and narrow and are available in various lengths.
Drop	These have a threading hole placed near the top of the bead.
Sequins	These are flat with a centre hole and are available in various sizes.

Marking

Mark the outline of the decoration on the RS of the garment using chalk, fabric marker, or tacking thread.

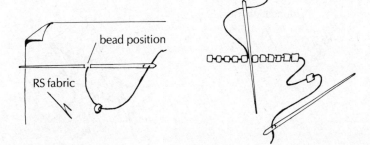

Figure 148   Figure 149

Applying the beads

Beads applied singly
Sew each bead bringing the needle through to the RS of the work, pick up a bead, take the thread to the WS of the work and secure with a small back stitch (see Figure 148).

Beads applied on a thread
Couching is a means of holding a decoration on to a fabric. Beads applied in rows can be held in this way.

Use two threaded needles. Bring up the first needle to the RS of the work, pick up several beads and secure the needle in the fabric so that the beads cannot move around or slip off. Take the second needle and thread and couch down the strung beads by taking a small stitch between every two or three beads. When the design line is completed fasten off the holding thread and the couching thread securely (see Figure 149).

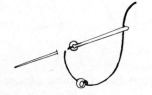

Figure 150

Sequins applied singly
There are two methods of applying sequins singly.

1 Apply each sequin with a back stitch making a stitch that equals half the diameter of the sequin (see Figure 150).
2 Centre a bead on each sequin by bringing the needle upwards through the centre of the sequin and the bead, and then down through the centre of the sequin. Fasten off securely on the underside of the fabric (see Figure 151).

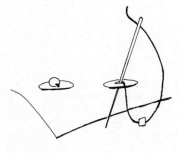

Figure 151

Sequins applied as a prestrung strip
Bring the needle up to the RS of the fabric between the first two sequins. Take a small stitch through the foundation

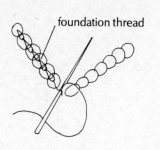

foundation thread

Figure 152

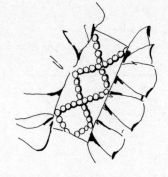

Figure 153   *Beaded cuff*

threads at the back of the sequins. Repeat this process, catching the foundation threads down at every third sequin. Finish off with two or three back stitches on the underside of the fabric (see Figure 152).

Figure 154   *Evening blouse border decorated with beads and sequins*

Chapter 12
BRAIDS AND FRINGES

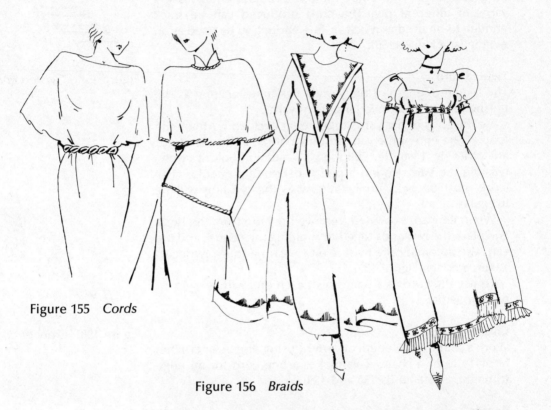

Figure 155   *Cords*

Figure 156   *Braids*

Braids are used in a number of ways on many types of garment. They may be used to bring contrast in colour and texture so adding interest to style lines and edges.

A braid is a narrow strip of a required length. It can be made from a variety of yarns to produce different colour detail and texture variations.

There are a number of different ways of constructing braids which can be divided into two groups:

1   Using a continuous yarn worked with the necessary tools such as crochet hooks, tatting shuttles, and knitting needles.

2   Yarns cut to required lengths which must be calculated depending upon the length of braid required and the type of construction used. A small sample of the braid must be worked to estimate the amount of yarn required for the appropriate length.

Cords

This is one of the simplest ways of producing a braid trimming. The cord is varied by the use of colour and by using yarns of different ply. The cord produced can be thick enough to be used as a belt or fine enough to be used as an edging (see Figure 155).

Twisted cord

The required length of the yarn is five times as long as the finished length. Cut two lengths of yarn.

Tie the ends of the yarns together at each end. Attach the loop at one end of the yarn around a hook, a door knob, or any other rigid handle. Pull the yarn taut and hold it firmly, twisting the yarns round a pencil or knitting needle. (The work must be held firmly otherwise the twisting will be irregular.)

When the yarn is twisted, remove the loop from the hook and place the two ends together, holding the centre, and the yarn will automatically twist itself to form a four-ply decorative cord (see Figure 157).

To use the cord as a belt, finish each end with tassels for tying together.

Chained cords

Work a continuous length of yarn by using fingers or crochet hook to form a chain. This makes a fine cord for an edge trimming (see Figures 158 and 159).

Braids

Method 1: plaiting

The number of yarns used determines the type of braid made and the finished result.

Three yarns

This is the most familiar plait and can be worked with many yarn combinations to make attractive braids. Colour variations (which in certain yarns will give a 'tweedy' look), metallic yarns, different textures, and beads and sequins can all be used.

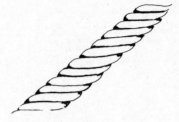

Figure 157   *Twisted cord*

Figure 158   *Crochet chain*

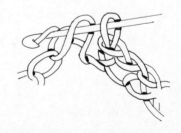

Figure 159   *Double crochet cord*

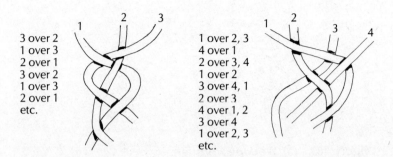

3 over 2	1 over 2, 3
1 over 3	4 over 1
2 over 1	2 over 3, 4
3 over 2	1 over 2
1 over 3	3 over 4, 1
2 over 1	2 over 3
etc.	4 over 1, 2
	3 over 4
	1 over 2, 3
	etc.

Figure 160 (left) *Sequence of yarn movement – three plait*

Figure 161 (right) *Sequence of yarn movement – four plait*

The three-yarn plait is so formed that one yarn can be drawn up to give a loose weave. This additional process must be taken into consideration in estimating the length required, as the drawing up process shortens the plait by approximately one-third its length.

Figure 160 shows the yarn movement sequence that forms a three-yarn plait.

To draw up, take yarn number 2 and pull it gently, easing the plait upwards keeping the loops evenly spaced.

Four yarns
Using yarns of constrasting colours forms a distinctive pattern repeat running through this plaited braid.

Figure 161 shows the method of four-yarn plaiting.

Up to seven or eight yarns can be used for plaiting to give wide chunky braids.

Method 2: knotting
Measure the yarns to twice the finished lengths required. To work accurately, and to produce an even texture, the cord must be mounted on to a holding line to support the braid. This can be in the form of a thick yarn attached to a board or a length of dowelling stapled to a board. A holding line of 8–10 cm is required to work a narrow braid. The yarns are mounted on to the centre of the holding line in the following way.

Fold the yarn in half, insert the looped end underneath the holding line and bring the two loose ends over the holding line and through the loop (see Figure 162).

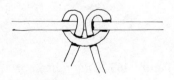

Figure 162

There are two simple knots which give a number of variations for different braid patterns.

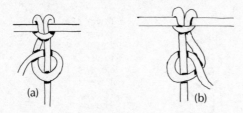

Figure 163   (a) *Working from left*
              (b) *Working from right*

Half hitch knot

This knot is worked from either the left or the right using two yarns (see Figure 163(a) and (b)).

Working from the left, the right-hand yarn must be held taut. Pass the left-hand yarn in front of it, then upwards and under it, bringing the loose end through the formed loop. Once the knot is completed the yarn must be pulled firmly to tighten. This tension must be kept uniform when forming the braid.

To work from the right, the left-hand yarn must be held taut while the same knotting pattern is carried out. This knot can be worked alternately to make an interesting pattern.

Flat knot

This knot is formed by using four yarns which are mounted on to the supporting line (see Figure 164).

The two inside yarns form the core of the braid (B and C) and must be kept taut. The two outside yarns (A and D) are used as tying yarns forming the knots as the braid is worked.

Take the left-hand yarn (A) underneath B and C and over the right-hand yarn (D). Then take the right-hand yarn over B and C and under the left-hand yarn (A). Pull the yarns firmly into place to adjust the tension. This process forms half the knot (see Figure 165).

To complete the knot, work the same process working from left to right. Take the right-hand yarn underneath B and C, and over the left-hand yarn. Then take the left-hand yarn over B and C and under the right-hand yarn (see Figure 166).

Practise both the half hitch knot and the flat knot, trying variations of patterns, yarn thicknesses and colours to make interesting braids (see Figure 167).

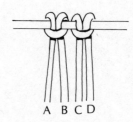

A B C D

Figure 164

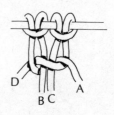

Figure 165   *First half knot*

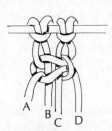
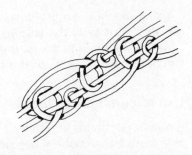

Figure 166 (left)   *Second half knot to complete flat knot*

Figure 167 (right)   *Braid formed by alternative pattern using four yarns*

Weaving

It is possible to produce a braid by the simple method of plain weaving without using a loom. The warp yarns are cut to the required length for the braid and must be supported and held taut. The number of yarns used determines the width of the braid (see Figure 168).

The weaving of the weft threads is a basic process of over and under each warp thread (see Figure 169). Tension must be even throughout the whole length of the braid otherwise there is distortion in the width of the braid.

A variety of colour and texture combinations can be used.

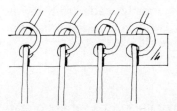

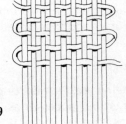

Figure 168   Figure 169

Fabric braid

This braid is made from fabric pieces used for making up a garment. Alternatively, a contrasting coloured fabric of similar weight can be used.

Cut a strip of fabric on the straight grain – length required by 0.5–1.5 cm, depending upon the use of the braid. Cut a matching sized strip in lightweight iron-on interfacing. Press the interfacing on the WS of the fabric.

Using machine embroidery, scallop stitch both edges of the strip. Cut away the surplus fabric (see Figure 170).

Attach the braid to the garment, catching down with small stitches on both edges of the braid (see Figure 171).

Use of commercial braids

A number of braids of different widths and textures are available from haberdashery departments. The following braids are illustrated in Figure 172.

1 Metallic, beaded, sequins make up decorative braids with a jewelled effect. Apply by hand making sure that the sequins or beads are not broken. See Figure 172(a).
2 A braid with a serrated edge made in various widths. Used as a decorative detail and is especially useful to use on children's clothing. The braid is attached by machine stitching along the centre of the braid. It can be applied flat or set into a seam. See Figure 172(b).
3 A flat braid with a worked appearance approximately 2 cm wide. Used as an edge finish on reversible coats and capes. The braid is attached by stitching close to the edge of the braid by machine stitching or hand stitching. It can also be used flat. See Figure 172(c).
4 A very narrow braid used for decorative purposes, 0.3 cm wide, with a rounded shape. It is useful for working curved areas. Applied by hand stitching. Couching the braid gives an attractive finish. See Figure 172(d).
5 A braid with a glossy finish, mostly made from rayon, approximately 0.5 cm wide. Used as an edge finish, for loops and frog fastenings. See Figure 172(e).

Fringing

Fringing makes a decorative edge finish to a variety of garments and accessories. The fringing can be a self-fabric decoration or it can be made up of a variety of colours, textures and yarn types. It is possible to buy ready-made fringes but this can work out expensive and the choice is limited.

Ideas can be developed to make fringes to add interest and individuality to garments and accessories using the basic skills of fringe making.

Self-fabric fringe
When cutting out the garment it is necessary to lengthen the pattern pieces to add on the fringing, for example, the bot-

Figure 170

Figure 171   *Fabric braid*

Figure 172

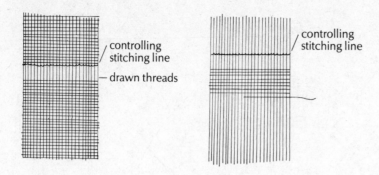

Figure 173

Figure 174

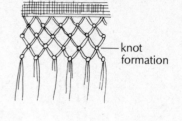

Figure 175

tom edge of a coat. Decide upon the depth of the fringe and add that measurement to the length of the pattern. This type of fringe can only be used on plain weave fabrics which are coarsely woven. Too fine a fabric will not always fray easily.

Trim the fabric edge on the grain line. Measure the depth of the fringe required from the bottom edge of the fabric and draw out two threads. Machine stitch a line of stitching just above the pulled threads. This can be a straight stitch, zig-zag stitch or an embroidery stitch. This row of stitching will control the fabric and prevent further ravelling of the fabric (see Figure 173).

Starting at the edge of the fringe, pull the threads to the line of stitching. A deep fringe can be knotted to give a different finish. Knotting the threads together also gives further control to the finished fringe (see Figures 174 and 175).

Knotted fringe

The edge of the garment or accessory must have a narrow hem finish of no more than 3–5 mm deep. The hem can be rolled or neatened with an invisible finish by slip hemming neatly. The hem must be neatened and pressed before the fringe is added. The knotted fringe is applied with a crochet hook.

Method

Cut a cardboard gauge 1 cm longer than the finished fringe to allow for the take-up of the knot. Wind the yarn around the gauge. Check the tension so that the strands are equal in length. Cut through the yarn at point A (see Figure 176).

Insert the crochet hook into the neatened fabric edge from the underside to the topside of the fabric. Hold the yarns at the cut edges and pull the loop through (see Figure 177).

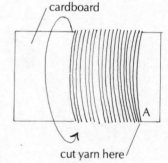

Figure 176

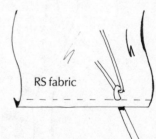

Figure 177

Draw the strands through the loop and tighten them up as the work progresses. The strands must be evenly spaced about 5 mm apart (see Figure 178).

The fabric can be held taut by lying the work flat on a table and weighting it down while the fringing is being applied to the finished edge.

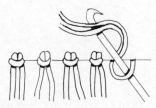

Figure 178

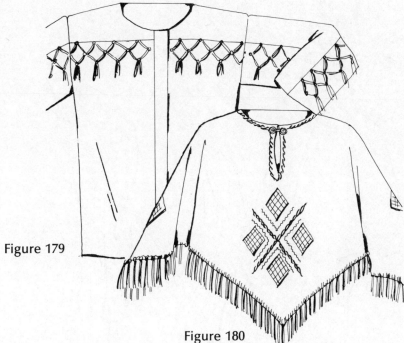

Figure 179

Figure 180

Chapter 13
FRILLS AND FLOUNCES

Figure 181 *Double frill .*   Figure 182 *Frills*

The addition of a frill or a flounce to certain garments brings a soft flowing line which is very flattering. A frill or flounce worn at the neckline of a blouse makes a very acceptable accessory to wear with a tailored suit. It fills in a neckline in a very attractive way. Certain fabrics lend themselves to this sort of decorative detail and the fineness of the fabric determines the amount of fullness the frill or flounce will take.

Frills

The amount of fabric required is up to three times the length of the frill by the depth of frill plus the seam allowance.

The amount of fullness depends upon the fabric being worked. Fine fabrics can take up to three times the length of the frill giving a very full frill. Medium-weight fabrics will take twice the length of the frill to give average fullness. Less fullness added would give just a little gathering.

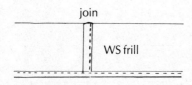

Figure 183

Making up
Any joins made in the frill must be unobtrusive. If the join is made on the selvedge a narrow open seam is suitable, otherwise a machine fell seam would be the most suitable as it is a flat seam.

Turn up a narrow hem and neaten according to the fabric being worked (see Figure 183).

Gathering and setting
Place two rows of gathering stitches at the top edge of the frill. Adjust the gathers. Mark four equal parts to place the frill accurately to the corresponding piece (see Figure 184).

Place the gathered edge to the corresponding piece. Tack and machine stitch along the fitting line. Trim the seam allowance and neaten. Do not press over the gathers (see Figure 185).

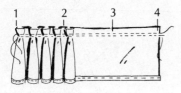

Figure 184

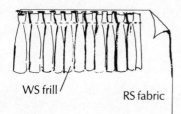

Figure 185

Figure 186 *Flounces*

Flounces

A flounce must be cut from soft fabric which falls naturally into folds. A flounce can be cut from a shaped pattern piece, from two circles, and can be cut to a full circle. A flounce gives flare at the hem line but keeps a smooth fitting line at the point at which it is attached to the garment.

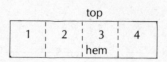

Figure 187

Making a pattern

Cut a rectangle the width of the flounce by the depth. Divide it into four equal parts (see Figure 187).

Slash and spread the fabric to introduce flare to the hem line (see Figure 188).

Outline the pattern shape. Cut out, label and add a seam allowance.

The amount of flare introduced by slashing and spreading depends upon the effect required. The pattern must be tested for fullness before cutting out in the garment fabric.

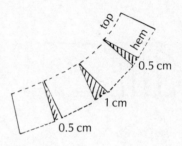

Figure 188

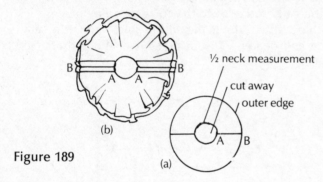

Figure 189

Cutting a pattern from a circle

Two circles are used to make a flounce for a neck line or sleeve decoration – (no seams are allowed) (Figure 189(a) and (b)):

Circle A = ½ neck line circumference
A–B   = depth of flounce
Circle B = outer edge of flounce

Cut out *two* circles in fabric. Cut through at line AB (Figure 189(a)). Join the two circles together at AB to make the flounce (Figure 189(b)).

Attaching flounce to garment

Before attaching the flounce neaten the flared edge with a narrow hem or a decorative edge finish.

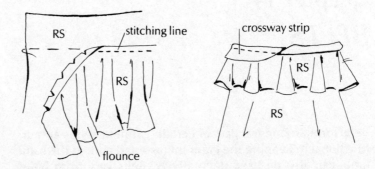

Figure 190   Figure 191

Attach the top edge to the corresponding piece by either of the following methods, depending upon the position of the flounce on the garment:

1   Clip the top edge of the flounce to the fitting line. Turn the seam allowance to the WS. Place the flounce to the corresponding fitting line. Tack and machine stitch in place (see Figure 190).

2   Place the top edge of the flounce to the corresponding piece, WS flounce to RS garment. Neaten the edge using a crossway strip to make a narrow binding (see Figure 191).

Chapter 14
BELTS

Belts form an integral part of certain garment styles and are functional in keeping the garment fastened and, at the same time, can also be used decoratively. Belts vary from being very narrow to a very wide cummerbund style. It is often assumed that a belt is just an 'extra' part of a dress in the form of a fastening, but as a fashion accessory a belt can be used to highlight a feature of a garment either in style, colour or texture. A belt is also a very useful accessory to give 'new life' to an already worn garment.

Accuracy is essential in belt making because any distortion, however slight, will cause the belt to crease or twist so that it does not sit comfortably on the wearer.

The width and style of the belt depends upon a number of factors:

1 *Fabric used* Interfacing is sometimes necessary to support certain fabrics. Sheer fabrics need backing otherwise raw edges are seen on the RS of the belt. Heavy-weight fabrics would add too much bulk to a narrow belt so it is wiser to use a minimum of 3 cm width when working with a heavy or bulky fabric, using a finer fabric as a lining.
2 *Style of garment* If the line is straight and sleek, asymmetrical, princess, or empire, a belt will alter the overall effect required. The addition of a belt must be looked at *on* the figure to see the line clearly and to determine whether the style line is broken in such a way that the belt detracts from the elegance of the original line.
3 *Figure type* Belts cut the figure crosswise so they will automatically shorten the appearance of the figure. A wide belt will shorten it even more. Belts worn at hip level are not suitable for a figure with a large hip measurement as this will draw attention to the figure at that point.

The length of the belt is important too, allowing it to fasten comfortably.

A tie belt must be long enough to allow the tie to hang attractively when tied. A guide for this measurement is: waist measurement plus 50 cm, depending upon the length of the garment from waist to hem. An overlap which is too short gives an unfinished look and with any energetic movement, or any strain, the belt could easily slip through the buckle and fall off the figure. An overlap which is too long looks untidy and adds bulk to a waist line appearance.

In making up it is essential to measure and to cut accurately on the grain.

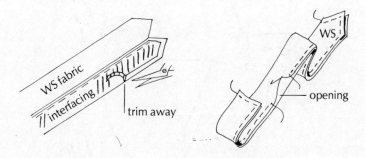

Figure 192   Figure 193

Figure 194

Belt with buckle fastening

The basic measurements required are: waist plus 15 cm overlap plus 2.5 cm buckle wrap plus seam allowance by twice depth plus seam allowance.

Cut out one length in fabric. Cut out one length of the belt interfacing half the width of the fabric strip. Cut the pointed end of the fabric and the interfacing (see Figure 192).

Place the interfacing to the fold of the fabric and tack just below the centre fold line. Fold the belt lengthwise placing the RS together. Machine stitch along the outer edge seam line leaving an opening of 10–12 cm long for turning the belt to the RS (see Figure 193).

Figure 195

Trim down and grade the seam allowance. Trim away the interfacing to the stitching line to reduce the bulk inside the belt. Turn the belt to the RS and press. Slip stitch the edges of the opening together. Topstitch 0.5 cm from all edges of the belt before removing the tacking from centre line (see Figure 194).

Attach the buckle to the straight end of the belt, taking the belt over the centre prong. Sew securely in place (see Figure 195).

Punch eyelets in the pointed end of the belt if the buckle has a prong. The eyelets should be evenly spaced. Check the waist measurement to position the first eyelet hole.

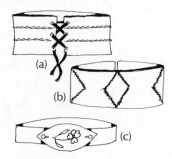

Figure 196

The belts shown in Figures 196 and 197 provide variation in

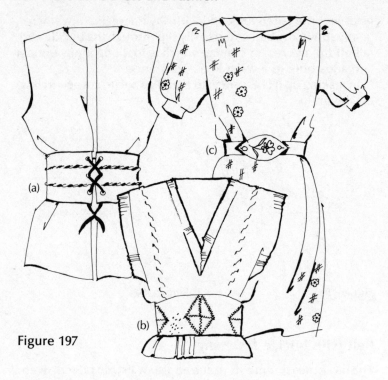

Figure 197

the range of basic techniques and can be used to create decorative ideas linking up with the functional use of a belt in relation to the garment it is to be worn with.

Belt 1 (Figure 197(a))

Materials
Suitable fabric: firm cotton, close weave
Main fabric: 2 lengths (waist measurement by 2 cm plus seam allowance)
Contrasting fabric: 1 length (waist measurement by 2 cm plus seam allowance)
No. 3 cord (contrasting colour): 2 lengths (as for fabric plus 1 cm)
Backing fabric: 1 length (waist measurement by 6 cm plus seam allowance)
Firm interfacing: 1 length (waist measurement by 6 cm plus seam allowance)
No. 3 cord for lacing: 1 length (approximately 50 cm)
Sewing thread

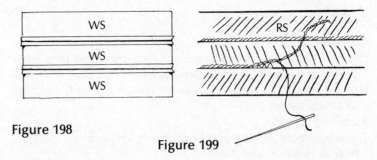

Figure 198

Figure 199

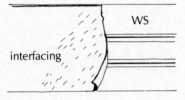

Figure 200

Making up

Join the three top fabric strips together lengthwise. Press the seams open (see Figure 198).

Sew the cord to the seam lines, attaching it with small stitches on the underside of the cord (see Figure 199).

Tack the interfacing to the WS of the belt (see Figure 200). Place the belt lining to the belt, RS together. Machine stitch from A to B (see Figure 201).

Turn the belt to the RS through the opening at AB. Close the opening neatly with small firm stitches.

Press the belt lightly on the underside. Using a stiletto, punch holes and insert eyelets at regular intervals (0.5 cm) from the CF of the belt. Thread the cord through the eyelet holes to fasten the belt. Finish the ends of the cord by knotting (see Figure 202).

Various colour and texture combinations may be used for this belt.

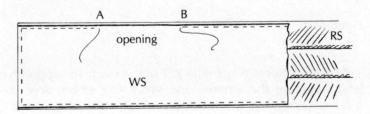

Figure 201

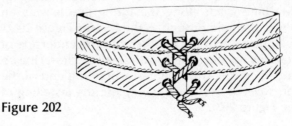

Figure 202

Belt 2 (Figure 197(b))

Materials
Cream wool fabric, plain weave: 2 lengths (waist measurement by 6 cm plus seam allowance)
Firm interfacing: 1 length (waist measurement by 6 cm plus seam allowance)
Matching thread
Tapestry wools (toning and contrasting colours)
3 button moulds (size 1 cm)

Making up
Take one length of fabric. Mark the CF and the SS with tailor tacks (see Figure 203).

Using plain paper cut a pattern to belt size and work out a decorative detail for embroidery (see Figure 204).

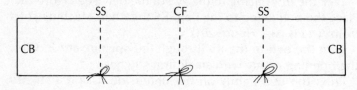

Figure 203

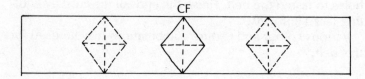

Figure 204

Attach the interfacing to the WS of the fabric to support it while working the embroidery. Work the embroidery at intervals along the whole length of the belt. Make fabric loops for the CB fastening. Attach loops to the belt (see Figure 205).

Place the topside of the belt to the underside, placing RS together. Machine stitch along the fitting line leaving an opening to turn the belt through to the RS (see Figure 206).

Pull the belt through to the RS. Press on the underside of the belt. Close the opening neatly with small stitches. Line up the loops at CB closing with the corresponding end of the belt. Sew on covered buttons to complete the fastening of the belt (see Figure 207).

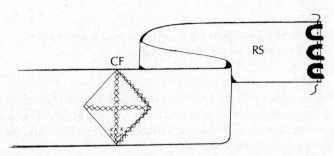

Figure 205

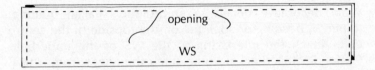

Figure 206

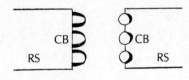

Figure 207

The embroidery on this belt must be bold in design. Cross stitch is a useful stitch to form an attractive pattern. It is essential to do experimental work before finally deciding upon the embroidery used and to make sure that the decorative work is balanced in relation to the width and length of the belt.

Belt 3 (Figure 197(c))

This belt is made up of a shaped front panel and is particularly attractive if worn with a princess line dress, lining up the belt with the dress fitting lines.

Measure accurately when making the belt pattern to make sure that the fitting lines match up and that the belt size is in proportion to give a pleasing finish.

Measurements
Piece 1: measure from panel line A round the back of the figure to panel line B.
Piece 2: measure across the front of the figure from A to B (see Figure 208).

Materials
Medium dressweight fabric
Firm interfacing

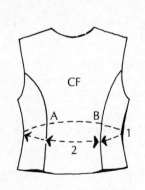

Figure 208

Piece 1
Cut in fabric 2 lengths by 4 cm plus seam allowance.
  Cut 1 length in firm interfacing.

Piece 2
Make a paper pattern to form a decorative detail panel, grading the shape from 4 cm at each side to 7 cm at CF. (These are approximate measurements. Personal design lines and detail might require otherwise.)
  Cut 2 pieces in fabric.
  Cut 1 piece in firm interfacing.

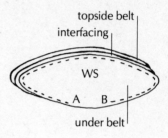

Figure 209

Making up
Work decorative details in embroidery, Italian quilting, trapunto, beading or appliqué on the topside of the centre belt. Attach the interfacing to the WS of the underbelt. Placing RS together, machine stitch the edges from A to B (see Figure 209).
  Make up piece 1. Attach the interfacing and machine stitch the edges, leaving an opening to pull it through to the RS. Turn pieces 1 and 2 to the RS and press. Work buttonholes and attach buttons, or attach decorative fastening to each side of the centre of the belt (see Figure 210).

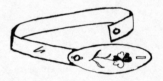

Figure 210

Figure 211   *Firm leather belt*   Figure 212   *Soft leather belt*

Leather and suede belts

Leather and suede are not difficult materials to work and it is possible to use both of them for belt making without using specific tools for leather work. The style of the belt will depend upon the weight of the skin being used (see Figures 211 and 212). It is possible to use very small pieces to bring a variety of shape and colour contrast into the belt design.

Leather and suede belts can be unlined or lined with a very thin skin or a petersham ribbon.

Unlined belt

This belt can be made from a piece of leather or suede in a variety of weights depending upon the effect required.

Decide upon the width of the belt and if working with a very soft skin, add 0.6 cm to the width to allow for a 0.3 cm hem along each edge.

A matching buckle is required which must be wide enough to take the fastened belt without creasing.

Making up

Cut a paper pattern – waist measurement plus 18 cm by width (The extra 18 cm is for a 3 cm buckle wrap and a 15 cm overlap.)

Place the pattern on to the WS of skin. Check that the thickness of the skin is even. Use weights to hold the pattern in place. Mark around the pattern with tailor's chalk. Cut it out using a pair of sharp scissors or a knife. Cut carefully to avoid a jagged edge to the cutting line. Machine stitch (using a leather machine needle) along the outer edges of the belt. Further rows of stitching can also be worked (see Figure 213).

Attach the buckle and fasten by stitching into place (see Figure 214). If the buckle has a prong, punch holes at waist measurement point and then at 3 cm intervals.

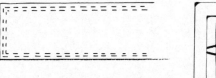

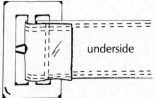

underside

Figure 213   Figure 214

Figure 215   Figure 216

Use of rouleau

The use of rouleau in belt making is shown in Figures 215 and 216.

Make up the rouleau to the width required joining, if necessary, to make up the required length. The joins on the crossway strips must be placed the same way (see Figure 217).

For evening and cocktail wear, silver or gold fabric can be introduced into a plaited or twisted rouleau.

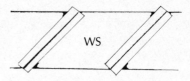

Figure 217

INDEX